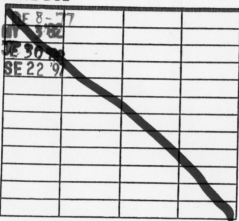

STATE LEGISLATIVE REDISTRICTING

Major Issues in the Wake of Judicial Decision

By

PAUL T. DAVID

and

RALPH EISENBERG

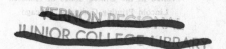

PUBLIC ADMINISTRATION SERVICE

1313 East 60th Street, Chicago 37, Illinois

Library of Congress Catalog Card No. 62-21670

Printed in the United States of America
Lincoln Printing Company, Chicago

PREFACE

This study was undertaken initially as a paper for presentation at the annual meeting of the American Political Science Association, September 5, 1962. The sources used were those available up to the end of August, 1962, which included the opinions for most of the relevant cases up to July 18, 1962, and news accounts for a number of additional court decisions of considerable importance that occurred in late July and August. Wherever possible, the texts of the opinions for these additional decisions were obtained, principally from the National Municipal League, and were examined during the period in which the study was going through press.

When the study was undertaken, it was assumed that most courts would be in recess during August and that any action affecting the 1962 elections would have become final by mid-July. The situation proved far more fluid than expected, and further events of consequence may occur before the study is published. Much as this may harass scholarship, it should encourage all friends of equitable representation in the affairs of government. Progress is being achieved more rapidly than anyone could have expected.

The authors have been engaged in research on problems of state legislative representation since 1960 under the auspices of the Bureau of Public Administration of the University of Virginia, which has published their previous studies entitled *Devaluation of the Urban and Suburban Vote,* Volumes I and II. The Bureau, of which Mr. Eisenberg is a staff member, provided assistance for the present study by permitting the authors to draw on its research files and other resources. The help provided by the Bureau is gratefully acknowledged, although it should be understood that the Bureau has no responsibility for the substantive conclusions of the present study.

Assistant Professor James J. Bolner of the University of Alabama assisted the authors in rechecking the documentation in the notes appended to the study. His help is gratefully acknowledged, as is also that of law student Michael L. Murray and of the staffs of the Law Library of the University of Virginia; the National Municipal League; and Congressional Quarterly, Inc.

PAUL T. DAVID
RALPH EISENBERG

University of Virginia
September 10, 1962

CONTENTS

CONTENTS

STATE LEGISLATIVE REDISTRICTING

Major Issues in the Wake of Judicial Decision

The decision by the United States Supreme Court on March 26, 1962, in the Tennessee reapportionment case, *Baker* v. *Carr*, has already assumed historic importance.[1] It may well mark a turning point in the evolution of American state legislatures and of state government generally. Important as the case seemed when it was decided, its potentialities have steadily increased in the months since the decision.

The Court held in *Baker* v. *Carr* that the federal courts have jurisdiction in cases involving inequity in state legislative representation. The standard imposed was no less and no more than the requirement of the Fourteenth Amendment of the United States Constitution, that no state shall "deny to any person within its jurisdiction the equal protection of the laws." The jurisdiction of the state courts was also extended by implication, and it has thus become the task of the state and federal courts to determine what constitutes "the equal protection of the laws" in arrangements for state legislative representation.

In announcing the decision, the Court provided a minimum of guidance beyond a full statement of the reasons why jurisdiction was being accepted. Justice Stewart, in a concurring opinion, spelled out the narrow scope of the Court's decision. Justice Clark, although also concurring, suggested that remarkably unequal arrangements for representation could be reconciled with "the equal protection of the laws" if they were part of a "rational" design.[2] The question of whose rationality and for what purpose was left open and has led to considerable confusion. Justices Frankfurter and Harlan in dissenting went to some length in attacking the whole decision. They argued that the courts were being saddled with an impossible task, and one that could only have disastrous effects upon the position of the judiciary.

Most observers have been surprised by what has happened in the interval since the decision. There was a predictable outburst of states' rights sentiment from a few highly placed spokesmen for that position, but the outburst was brief, found little public support, and has already dwindled to an occasional *pro forma* statement for the record. In most parts of the country the decision has had a generally favorable press.

What is more important, the decision has opened a round of constitutional litigation in state and federal courts that is probably without any

1

close parallel in the speed with which it has been initiated in a multiplicity of states. Complainants were in court filing new suits in additional states within hours after the Supreme Court's decision was announced, although on its face the decision affected only Tennessee. The speed with which the lower courts have acted has been a further source of surprise, in view of the lengthy delays that usually attend litigation on constitutional questions.

Some Highlights of Recent Developments

The situation has developed so rapidly in the months since the decision in March that it has been continuously difficult to arrive at any accurate summary of what has happened. About half of the states have been involved so far in litigation challenging their existing arrangements in the light of *Baker* v. *Carr*. Existing state legislative apportionments have been invalidated or substantially so in at least 14 states. Federal courts acted in 5 of these states: Alabama,[3] Georgia,[4] Tennessee,[5] Florida,[6] and Oklahoma.[7] State courts acted in 9 states: Vermont,[8] Rhode Island,[9] Maryland,[10] Michigan,[11] Kansas,[12] North Dakota,[13] Mississippi,[14] Idaho,[15] and Pennsylvania.[16] State constitutional provisions on legislative representation apparently have been invalidated as contrary to the requirements of the Fourteenth Amendment in at least 6 states. The decision was by the federal courts in Georgia, Florida, and Oklahoma; similar decisions were reached in state courts in Rhode Island, Maryland, and Michigan.

The invalidation of an existing apportionment does not immediately produce a substitute. In several instances, legislatures have been put under notice to act at their next regular sessions or in special sessions. At the time of the ultimate reckoning, these states may appeal the invalidating decisions, if they have not already done so, or they may wait until courts attempt alternative action after the political limits of legislative action have been tested. But already new districting arrangements are in effect for the elections in November, 1962, in Alabama,[17] Tennessee,[18] and Maryland.[19] Legislatures in several states were in session in July and August to work on reapportionment schemes that will probably be subject to further consideration in the courts.

The process of litigation is still spreading rapidly. It seems entirely likely that litigation to test the federal constitutionality of existing arrangements will be initiated in most of the states within the next few months. As experience accumulates and the documents become available, it becomes progressively easier to draft the petitions and briefs. There is a prima facie basis for getting a case into court in almost every state, particularly in view of the idiosyncratic aspects of the districting arrangements that can be found in almost every state. Even the states that rank highest on the quantitative measures of fairness in state legislative representation usually include some districts where existing arrangements are difficult to justify or defend.[20]

The wave of litigation that began in the wake of the Supreme Court decision came on so rapidly because there was a genuine desire in many states to secure relief in time to have it effective in the 1962 elections. With that objective, time was obviously of the essence.

Perhaps the most striking proceedings were those in Alabama, where a three-judge federal court took charge with unusual vigor. On April 14, in *Sims* v. *Frink*, the court gave the legislature until July 16 to act at least to the extent required by existing but long disregarded state constitutional provisions.[21] The legislature was then convened and did act by July 21, but mainly in the form of proposed state constitutional amendments that would not have been effective until the elections of 1966, although a statutory "stand-by" plan was provided that also would have become effective only in 1966. The court then worked selectively to give temporary approval on July 25 to the proposed amendment plan for the lower house and the proposed stand-by plan for the upper house, choosing for each house the plan closest to equality of representation—and then ordered the combined new plan into service for the elections of the present year. This was "the first time that a federal court has ever actually reapportioned a legislature," according to *Congressional Quarterly Weekly Report*.[22] No appeal was taken by the state, and a belated attempt by others to secure a stay from Supreme Court Justice Hugo L. Black was unsuccessful. Special primary elections are being held where required under special legislation. The court's order has thus become the actual basis for the election in 1962. The newly elected legislature, in which urban interests will have substantially increased representation, will meet under a warning from the court to complete the task of providing a more equitable plan of representation. Meanwhile, the court has retained jurisdiction, stating that if the new legislature does not act to provide an apportionment giving plaintiffs the equal protection of the laws, the court will do so.[23]

In most instances the courts have not been willing to move quite so firmly in the face of legislative opposition as the federal court in Alabama, but there have been repeated instances in which the legislatures were given specific periods within which to act. In Georgia, the legislature acted under pressure in April to revise the county unit system to provide somewhat less inequity in party primaries—and then saw its revised system invalidated on April 28, 1962, in *Sanders* v. *Gray*, along with the pre-vious system.[24] The result is that no unit system is in effect in the Georgia primaries for the 1962 election; for the first time in a half century, urban candidates have a reasonable opportunity to secure nomination and all voters are receiving equal treatment in the statewide primary.[25] The deci-sion has been appealed, but for political reasons as well as legal, a restoration of Georgia's nearly unique system for rural control of party primaries seems unlikely.[26]

In another Georgia case, *Toombs* v. *Fortson*, a somewhat different three-judge federal court on May 25 called for the early reapportionment of at least one house of the Georgia general assembly.[27] When the legislature failed to act in pursuance of the court's invalidation of existing provisions of the Georgia Constitution, the three judges split on what to do next. Two of them backed down, on July 18, so far as immediate action was concerned, with the result that the existing apportionment may still remain for the election in 1962. On September 6, however, the court is reported as having provided a further decision, that may become some-thing of a landmark, in which it held that both houses must be appor-tioned on a population basis. The court also rejected a proposal for a state constitutional amendment under which each county would have been assured a minimum of one member of the lower house.[28]

In Tennessee, where it was necessary to wait until April 23 for the mandate in *Baker* v. *Carr* to come back from the Supreme Court (unlike Alabama and Georgia where the lower federal courts could move imme-diately), the legislature was convened by the governor and redistricted both houses to some extent in June. The federal court then found that the new plan for the lower house still contained inequities and that the upper house plan was completely devoid of rationality. But the court concluded on June 22 that the "expedient course" was to permit the new plan to come into effect for one election, retaining jurisdiction and giving the next legislature until June 3, 1963, to act.[29]

Maryland provides another case, in this instance by state court action, in which the legislature has acted under pressure to redistrict one house on a basis that will be effective in 1962, while argument continues in regard to the other house.[30] In Michigan, in *Scholle* v. *Hare* on remand, the state Supreme Court ordered action effective in 1962, but its decision was stayed by Supreme Court Justice Potter Stewart on July 27.[31]

In Wisconsin, on June 13, a three-judge federal court ordered imme-diate action to redistrict, but after complicated proceedings in which the governor vetoed the work of his reconvened legislature and a special master was unable to bring in more than a mixed report, on August 15 the court dismissed the case for the time being.[32]

In Florida, a three-judge federal court ordered prompt action on July 23. One Florida legislator responded that the federal courts should "go straight to hell,"[33] but on August 11 the Florida legislature completed action to reapportion both houses, attempting, however, to make its action subject to voter approval on November 6. Further hearings in court were scheduled for August 20; and on September 5, the court was reported as having approved the legislature's plan for submitting a proposed constitutional amendment to the voters. The size of both houses would be increased, if the voters approve, with the additional seats going mainly to urban areas. The court retained jurisdiction while awaiting the outcome of the election.[34]

In Oklahoma, on August 3, a three-judge federal court handed down one of the most far-reaching decisions so far given, but gave the legislature until March 8, 1963, to reapportion both houses strictly on the basis of population.[35]

But in New York, a three-judge federal court that had refused action last January in *WMCA* v. *Simon* received the case back from the Supreme Court on June 11 and heard further argument on August 1; and on August 17, it again dismissed the suit in a unanimous action that will doubtless again be appealed.[36]

The consequences for state politics and government of decisions that will be effective in the 1962 elections will obviously be substantial in Alabama, Georgia, Tennessee, and Maryland. Changes as great or greater are in prospect in several other states, most notably Florida, Oklahoma, Mississippi, Rhode Island, and Kansas. Some degree of change may occur as the result of *Baker* v. *Carr* in more than half of the states before nominations are made for the state elections of 1964.

The form and extent of the prospective changes will be highly contingent on what is still to be done on issues not yet resolved. Obviously, much will depend on what the Supreme Court does with the lower court decisions that come up to it. Meanwhile, the substantive issues will continue to be debated in the lower courts and in the forums of public opinion.

Bicameral Differences and So-Called Federal Plans

The foggiest issue is the one on which the state courts divided in Maryland and Michigan: the extent to which, in a two-house state legislature, a looser standard of equality in representation may be used for one house than the other. In *Baker* v. *Carr*, the majority opinion drew no distinction between the two houses of a state legislature. Under the Tennessee Constitution, both houses are supposed to be apportioned primarily on the basis of the numbers of qualified voters. The issue of bicameral differences was therefore not posed directly in that case. Various commentators suggested, nonetheless, that in many states the sweep of the decision would probably be limited in practice to only a single house of the legislature. The precedent of the arrangements embodied in the federal Constitution was repeatedly cited by governors, judges, and editorial writers.

On April 23, 1962, however, the Supreme Court acted on a case in which the issue of bicameral differences was squarely involved. This was the Michigan case, *Scholle* v. *Hare*,[37] in which a state Supreme Court decision was sent back to the state for further action in the light of *Baker* v. *Carr*. Michigan has had, since 1952, a so-called federal plan under which the upper house districts were established on a fixed basis by state constitutional amendment. The upper house districts admittedly have no relationship to population. The state court had been urged to invalidate these provisions and had concluded that it lacked jurisdiction. It was the purpose of the Supreme Court on April 23, by a vote of seven to one, to assure the state court that it did indeed have jurisdiction. Two of the concurring justices, however, Justices Clark and Stewart, noted that "it may well turn out that the assertion of invidious discrimination is not borne out by the record."[38]

The Michigan court then decided on July 18, 1962, by a four to three vote, that the existing upper house provisions of the Michigan Constitution were invalid. The decision was promptly appealed and Justice Stewart entered a stay on July 27. According to *Congressional Quarterly Weekly Report*, Justice Stewart posed the issue as follows: Does the equal protection clause of the Fourteenth Amendment require the electoral districts of both houses of a bicameral state legislature to be based wholly on population? He indicated that he thought a state would have a right to establish one house on some other basis than population alone. The Michigan ruling if upheld, he thought, could result in change in more than 40 of the 49 bicameral state legislatures.[39]

These potentialities were equally apparent when the Michigan case was sent back to the state in April under circumstances in which the Supreme Court could instead merely have dismissed it.[40] The decision by the Supreme Court in *Scholle* v. *Hare* in April was a shock to all believers in federal plans at the state level, as well as to those who have tended to believe that, for this kind of issue, state constitutional provisions adopted by popular majorities of recent date would be immune to challenge on Fourteenth Amendment grounds. In a first reaction to the decision of April 23 by which the case went back to Michigan, the *Washington Post*, for example, commented editorially on April 25 as follows:

> It would be surprising indeed if the courts should interfere with the distribution of state Senate seats on a rational geographic basis in accord with the constitutional pattern for the United States Senate.

The *Post* reconsidered this view within a few days and has since argued the irrelevance of federal plans at the state level,[41] but it was undoubtedly voicing a widely held view in its earlier statement.

Contemporaneously with the evolution of the Michigan case, a complex line of development was occurring on the same issue in Maryland. In one of the most important of the early decisions after *Baker* v. *Carr*, on April 25, the Maryland Court of Appeals directed a lower court to take such action as necessary to bring the state's legislative arrangements into accord with Fourteenth Amendment requirements.[42] The lower court was directed, if necessary, to invalidate the state's own constitutional provisions for both houses; the high court indicated in its comments that all of these provisions were probably invalid. Apportionment in both houses had been frozen under the Maryland Constitution, despite a pattern of representation in each that seemed grossly inequitable.

The lower court judge, O. Bowie Duckett, then invalidated the constitutional provisions for the lower house only and the legislature redistricted the lower house on a compromise basis, effective in the forthcoming elections. Pressed to act further, on June 28, Judge Duckett again refused to act in regard to the upper house and defended his action on principles of federalism, leaving every county with a single state senator and the City of Baltimore with six. The City of Baltimore is an independent city, comparable to a county in its legal status, and the rational basis by which it can be allowed six state senators while the heavily populated suburban counties near it and Washington, D. C., can each continue with one is not readily apparent. Nevertheless, on appeal, Judge Duckett's decision was sustained by the Maryland high court by a vote of four to three on July 23; and that is the basis on which the Maryland case will presumably go to the Supreme Court of the United States.[43]

The Michigan and Maryland cases will provide opportunity for rulings in which the Supreme Court may have to come to terms with the issues of bicameral differences and so-called federal plans. The Court may find ways to dispose of these cases by ruling on issues narrower than those posed by Justice Potter Stewart in his New Hampshire vacation courtroom

8

in July.[44] But it would seem that both cases are at a point where some square ruling must eventually be forthcoming. As noted, they go in opposite directions, in each case by a state court vote of four to three.

Most political scientists and many other students of constitutional history undoubtedly believe that the attempt to use the federal precedent at the state level is invalid. As one of the present writers said in a letter that the *Washington Post* was kind enough to publish on April 29, 1962:

> Obviously some consideration should be given to existing political units and community relationships in drawing district lines, but the United States Senate is both irrelevant and improper as a model for representation within a state. It is irrelevant because a state is not a federal union of sovereign counties. It is improper, because where the Senate model has been used in the states, including Michigan, it has been used primarily and with quite deliberate intent as a facile means of practicing an invidious discrimination against city people. Such discrimination was no part of the intent when the United States Senate was created, and that body does not currently operate as a place in which any major category of citizens with definable interests is denied the equal protection of the laws.

In many states, the counties have some historic importance, but they are nonetheless creatures of the states. There is no apparent reason why every rural county is entitled to separate representation in either house of a state legislature, as states are entitled to representation in the federal Senate. In some states, there were practical reasons of convenience for giving each county the same representation a century ago, because all of the counties were roughly similar in size and population. With the long-term trend toward the concentration of population in urban areas, the county pattern of representation has become less appropriate, but has been maintained or even manipulated primarily to preserve the political power of rural interests.[45]

The general proposition that most of the states have imitated the federal arrangements seems to underlie much of the argument. The fact is, however, that the states have followed no uniform policy in devising legislative arrangements generally or in providing differing bases of representation in the two houses of a bicameral legislature. Prior to the decision in *Baker* v. *Carr*, there were only 16 states that had provided in their constitutions for the equivalent of the federal plan: a system in which in general one house was characterized by a fixed apportionment of representation among fixed districts with no regard for population and the other house was apportioned more or less on the basis of population. In 7 of these states, counties were treated like states in the federal union: every county received at least one representative in the lower house, and every county received the same representation in the upper house.

In a second group of 9 states, constitutional provisions contemplated an unqualified use of population as the basis for representation in one house and some kind of qualified population standard in the other house. Some of these states were close to the federal pattern. In California, for example, although population is specified as the primary criterion for the upper house, as it is for the lower, in the upper house no county may have more than one state senator, and not more than three counties may be combined in a single senate district. A single state senator thus represents Los Angeles County, with its current population of more than 6,000,000.

The other 25 states fall into two further groups. In one group of 16, population is the principal criterion for both houses, but is qualified in one way or another for both. In the other group of 9 states, population is the criterion for representation in the entire legislature without any substantial qualification by statute or constitution, whether the legislature consists of only one house, as in Nebraska, or of two, as in the other 8 states.

These figures are the count of the authors, based on state constitutions and statutes as they existed prior to *Baker* v. *Carr*. The states are identified in Table 1. Even the simple classification outlined is not easy to apply in view of the oddities of some state laws and constitutions; other students might classify some states differently.[46] The broad picture is certainly one of great diversity, but so far as any standard has received general allegiance in principle, it is the population criterion.

Thirty-four states used some form of population or the equivalent as an apportionment criterion for both chambers of the legislature. No state had completely rejected all pretense of using some form of population, however qualified, as an apportionment standard in at least one house. Only 16 states had committed themselves to disregard population entirely in the construction of legislative districts in one house. Eighteen states prescribed population without any qualifications as the apportionment standard for at least one legislative chamber, and 9 states provided this standard for their entire legislature.

The provisions just summarized are those that were supposed to be legally controlling prior to *Baker* v. *Carr*. Actually, practice lagged behind principle in many states because of the reluctance of state legislatures to carry out existing state constitutional provisions, or even to reapportion at all. So far as the actually prevailing differences between the two houses in a bicameral legislature were concerned, there were only 8 states in

March, 1962, in which one house was less than one-half as representative as the other: California, Connecticut, Missouri, Montana, Nevada, New Jersey, Rhode Island, and Vermont. In 11 other states, one house was between one-half and three-quarters as representative as the other: Alaska, Idaho, Illinois, Kansas, Michigan, New Mexico, North Carolina, Ohio, South Carolina, Utah, and Wyoming. In 26 states, one house was about as representative as the other, although the group included many states in which neither house was very representative.[47]

TABLE 1

Classification of States by Bases of Representation in Houses of the State Legislature, March, 1962[a]

Equivalent of "Federal" Plan	Population in One House, Qualified Population in Other	Qualified Population in Both Houses	Unqualified Population in Both Houses
Arizona	California	Alabama	Indiana
Arkansas	Kansas	Alaska	Kentucky
Connecticut[b]	Mississippi	Colorado	Massachusetts
Delaware[c]	Missouri	Florida	Minnesota
Hawaii	North Carolina	Georgia	Nebraska[d]
Idaho	Ohio	Iowa	South Dakota
Illinois	Oklahoma	Louisiana	Virginia
Maryland	Tennessee	Maine	Washington
Michigan	West Virginia	New Hampshire[e]	Wisconsin
Montana		New York	
Nevada		Oregon	
New Jersey		Pennsylvania	
New Mexico		Rhode Island	
North Dakota		Texas	
South Carolina		Utah	
Vermont[f]		Wyoming	

[a]Based on an inspection of state constitutions and laws; for further information see National Municipal League, *Compendium on Legislative Apportionment*, 2d ed., New York: January, 1962.

[b]Every town has one representative in the lower house and no town more than two; population is the standard for the upper house.

[c]Representation in both houses of the Delaware legislature has been frozen on a basis that has had little or no relation to population in recent years.

[d]Nebraska has only a single house, for which population without qualification is the standard for apportionment.

[e]The upper house is districted on the basis of tax payments, which have only indirect relation to population; the lower house is based on population with some qualification.

[f]Every town has one representative in the lower house; population is the standard for the upper house, except that each county must have a member.

It seems clear that there is no general precedent or custom in the state experience that requires the acceptance or maintenance of the so-called federal plan at the state level. In some instances where such a plan exists, as in the representation of the towns in Connecticut and Vermont, the practice is simply an anachronistic survival, long overdue for reform. The best known federal plans, such as those of California and Michigan,[48] are modern products of a situation in which rural interests saw danger that they would lose their pre-existing position of political power. An acceptance of gross over-representation of rural interests in one house was the price exacted for something approaching fair representation of urban interests in the other house. In the absence of any generally enforceable standard, blackmail was possible and, indeed, blackmail tactics were approximated in some states.

Bicameral differences less extreme than those provided by the so-called federal plans present somewhat different problems and are usually less offensive to normal conceptions of equity in representation. Many federal judges have therefore expressed views[49] similar to those summarized in early June by the Solicitor General, Archibald Cox. He referred to

> . . . the claims of historically separate units such as towns and counties to have equal recognition, the desirability of distributing political power geographically, the need to prevent a single large city or two from dominating an entire State; . . . I do not mean to suggest how the question should be decided, but it would not surprise me greatly if the Supreme Court were ultimately to hold that if seats in one branch of the legislature are apportioned in direct ratio to population, the allocation of seats in the upper branch may recognize historical, political and geographical subdivisions *provided that the departure from equal representation in proportion to the population is not too extreme.* But surely a very strong argument can also be made that there must be representation proportionate to population in at least one branch of the legislature.[50]

The rule suggested by the Solicitor General would represent a considerable advance over the conditions that have prevailed generally, but it nonetheless leaves unresolved the question of why, if equality is related to equity, equality should be limited to one house. Those who hold strongly the position to which he refers, to the effect that inequality is essential in at least one house in order to distribute political power geographically, would come into the court of public opinion with much cleaner hands if they were at least prepared to admit a principle of offsetting inequalities. There is no way by which a disproportionate amount of representation can be given to one group of voters without taking it away from another; but opposing inequalities in the two houses could be brought into balance. If it is necessary in some states, for example, to concede some degree of moderate over-representation for rural interests in one house, equity would suggest the necessity for a like amount of over-representation for urban interests in the other house.

As a practical matter, any rule other than the one of equality of representation in the legislature as a whole is deficient as an enforceable standard of equity. The suggestion by the Solicitor General could cause endless difficulty if the courts were to attempt to follow it. When does a departure from representation proportionate to population become "too extreme"? This is not a standard; it is the opposite, unless it is expanded by some further specification.

To the extent that the equal protection of the laws can be given content as a standard for representation, it would seem that the value of one voter's vote should be made as close to that of another as may be reasonably possible.[51] The most desirable way to achieve this goal is to provide equality of treatment in both houses. This is what is still prescribed in many state constitutions, as it was in many others at an earlier day.[52]

The goal of "a proportionate representation of the people in the legislature" is, in fact, one of the most ancient of the civil rights to which Americans have given allegiance. In the Northwest Ordinance, adopted by the United States in Congress assembled, July 13, 1787, the inhabitants of what was to become five states were assured in articles that were to "forever remain unalterable, unless by common consent," that

> The inhabitants of the said territory shall always be entitled to the benefits of the writ of *habeas corpus,* and of the trial by jury; of a proportionate representation of the people in the legislature; and of judicial proceedings according to the course of the common law.[53]

These provisions were adopted by the Congress during the period in which the federal convention was sitting for the purpose of writing our present Constitution. They were influential in shaping the provisions applicable to the United States House of Representatives,[54] and help to make it clear that the provisions adopted for the United States Senate were indeed a political compromise and not a standard of equity. The kind of standard intended by the Northwest Ordinance, which made no distinction between the houses of a legislature, was the kind to which the federal court in Oklahoma was returning in its opinion of August 3, 1962, in which it is said to have directed the legislature of Oklahoma to follow

> . . . the general principle of substantial numerical equality, to the end that each voter shall have the same power and influence in the election of members of the two houses.[55]

It is not possible to achieve equity in the total plan if inequality of treatment in one house is associated with no more than equality in the other. Despite the considerable efforts that have been made to read a double standard into the single criterion laid down by the Fourteenth Amendment, it would seem that citizens are entitled to the equal protection of the laws in the legislature as a whole and not merely in one house. The implications of this simple proposition have not been widely realized; but the longer the argument continues, the more obvious they may become.

What Constitutes Reasonable Equality of Representation?

Beyond the problem of bicameral differences, the second most important issue before the courts is what constitutes reasonable equality of representation in the situations where equality is the objective. Precise mathematical equality could be attained only if the arithmetical value of the vote as a proportionate share of state legislative representation could be brought to an identical level for all citizens. Practically, this is generally held to be impossible, and the courts have frequently said that precise mathematical equality is not necessary under a rule of reason.

The general use of a population standard neglects substantial variations in the proportion of the population that consists of adults of voting age. Even within those portions of the adult resident population that are legally qualified to vote, the use of the population standard neglects the wide variations in the proportions of persons qualified to vote who actually do so. From some points of view this neglect is justified and from others not. Nevertheless, the population standard has been generally regarded as the practical standard that most merits use.

The population standard has been widely qualified in practice, as already noted. Many of these qualifications seem invidiously discriminatory on their face. Only two of the commonest types are considered here: (1) those that impose maximum limits upon the amount of representation that may be accorded to any town, county, or city and (2) those that impose minimum requirements in regard to the representation that must be given each town or county.[56]

The maximum provisions are the ones that seem least defensible from any point of view. They embody most directly the concept that the voting power of large bodies of voters should be limited. This is another way of saying that voters of certain classes, defined by where they live, should each be given a devalued vote—a vote that gives each of them a smaller than average fraction of the voting power to which other voters are entitled. The result, in conjunction with other provisions, is the common situation in which the voters in the most populous counties have had a vote that is worth about three-quarters of the statewide average, whereas in the smallest counties the vote has been worth twice as much or more.

In recent research the authors have computed such vote values as averages for every county in the United States. A major portion of this research was published in December, 1961, by the Bureau of Public Administration, University of Virginia, in the report entitled *Devaluation of the Urban and Suburban Vote, A Statistical Investigation of Long-Term Trends in State Legislative Representation,* by Paul T. David and Ralph Eisenberg. Volume II of this report, which completes the county data for the years 1910, 1930, 1950, and 1960, was published in September, 1962, also by the Bureau of Public Administration, University of Virginia.

The maximum provisions are already beginning to receive rough treatment in the courts, particularly where they exist for both houses or for that house in which population is supposed to be the predominant standard by comparison with the other house. The maximums involved in the Georgia county unit plan were among the first to go.[57] In Georgia, a federal court also invalidated the state constitutional provisions for the lower house, which had contained a maximum of 3 seats for the most populous counties, although this action has not so far been made effective.[58] In Florida, the federal court in its decision of July 23 evidently invalidated the state constitutional maximum under which no county could receive more than 3 seats in the lower house, and perhaps also the maximum of 1 in the upper house.[59] In Oklahoma, the federal court decision of August 3 invalidated a state constitutional provision under which no county could receive more than 7 seats in the lower house of the state legislature. The court went on to direct the legislature to provide a plan by March 8, 1963, under which Oklahoma County would receive 19 seats and Tulsa County 15.[60] In Maryland, the lower house changes have involved invalidation of a state constitutional provision limiting any county to 6 seats in the lower house.[61]

The minimum provisions most often take the form of requiring that every county shall have at least 1 representative in the larger house of a two-house legislature. In the New England states of Connecticut, Rhode Island, and Vermont, a similar provision has prevailed for the towns. The extent to which such provisions provide representation above a simple population standard in the case of the smaller counties or towns depends upon the total geographic distribution of the state's population in relationship to the size of the legislative house concerned. Invariably there is some effect in the direction of rural over-representation, and a converse effect in the direction of under-representation for the more populous counties.

The view that every county should have at least 1 representative in one house dies hard in the states where it has become deeply imbedded in long practice and in state constitutional provisions. As might be supposed, courts have so far been less willing to deal vigorously with these situations than with the counterpart problem of the maximums. In Alabama, for example, the three-judge court allowed every county to retain 1 representative in the lower house, with the remaining seats distributed on a population basis as closely as possible. The result gives Jefferson County (Birmingham) 17 seats instead of its former 7 in the lower house, but only 16 per cent of the voting strength in the lower house instead of the 19 to which it would be entitled on a population basis.[62]

In Alabama, the depopulation of rural areas has not proceeded as far as it has in some states; the 1960 census reported no county with fewer than 10,000 inhabitants. In such states as Kansas and Oklahoma, the hastiest glance at the figures will reveal numerous counties under 10,000 population and many with as few as two, three, or four thousand inhabitants. Yet the governor of Oklahoma has complained of the recent decision because he had "always felt that every county should have one" member of the lower house in his state.[63] In Kansas, the state Supreme Court on July 30 entered a stay against a lower state court decision that evidently invalidated the provisions under which each Kansas county was guaranteed 1 member in the lower house.[64]

There are many states in which equitable apportionment will be impossible for the lower house unless the rule of 1 member for every county or town is abandoned. It would seem that when the courts have had time to consider the problem fully, many such rules will have to be abandoned. This means that in thinly populated areas, existing counties must be grouped to provide districts of reasonable size for even a single member. This is, of course, merely the rule that has usually been followed in composing upper house districts in most states and in composing congressional districts for the United States House of Representatives.

Political scientists would doubtless generally agree that many of the areas in question are long overdue for a substantial consolidation of counties into a much smaller number than presently exists. With enough county consolidation, a rule of at least 1 member for each county might conceivably be retained. It would seem, however, that the consolidation into a smaller number of legislative districts will have to come first if county consolidation for purposes of more effective local government is to come later or at all, for the heavy representation of outdated counties at state houses all over the country has been a prime reason for the failure of county consolidation movements, despite the fact that consolidation has been widely recognized as needed for at least 30 years.

In the states where a simple population standard exists in the state constitution without qualifying maximums or minimums for one house or both, application of the Fourteenth Amendment standard seems relatively simple. It involves no more than a decision concerning where and how widely the actual districting may vary from the population standard for reasons of legislative or administrative convenience without becoming invidiously discriminatory. Presumably the situation will become the same in states where maximums and minimums and similar qualifying restrictions are invalidated.

Efforts to devise a general rule for such circumstances have not been lacking. A committee of political scientists, reporting in 1951 on the congressional problem, suggested a statutory rule under which no district would be permitted to deviate from the population average by more than 10 or 15 per cent, thus permitting a spread in district size at most from 85 to 115 per cent of the average.[65] Bills to this effect have been repeatedly introduced in Congress by Representative Emanuel Celler; in recent years, his proposal has provided for a district population variance of not more than 20 per cent from the statewide average.[66]

More recently, Senator Joseph S. Clark, in a congressional bill that would set standards for state legislatures, has suggested a limit under which the population per representative would be no more than 50 per cent greater in one district than another.[67] Various judges have suggested a rule of thumb under which no single-member district should be more than twice as large as another. The three-judge federal court in Georgia that invalidated the county unit plan suggested a series of tests, some of which involved electoral college analogies.[68]

In a study of the problem of districting New York for state senators under various proposals for amending the state Constitution, Professor Ruth Silva has concluded that if county lines are respected in grouping small counties and dividing large ones, the smallest range of inequality between districts that can be achieved will be about 22 per cent—equivalent to the standard she expects the National Municipal League to recommend in its Model State Constitution.[69]

The main limitation of any such general rule is the possibility that it will be applied systematically to the benefit of one category of citizens, such as those living in rural areas, or systematically to the disadvantage of some other category, such as urban voters, in which case the result will probably be invidiously discriminatory to a rather high degree. Where reasonable equality of representation is the objective, it would seem essential to look directly at the facts of any challenged system and to ask a simple question, namely: Is there any reason why it would not have been equally convenient and appropriate to lay out a districting plan that would come closer to the objective of equality? If so, why should not the more appropriate plan be installed? Where a challenged plan shows clear evidence of discrimination against some definable category of citizens, as distinguished from a moderate amount of random variation arising from geographic factors, it would seem especially appropriate to hold the challenged plan invalid, even if the departure from some system of averages is not very great.

A different kind of a standard could be suggested that would be based on the statistical work that has gone into the determination for each state of the minimum percentage of the population that can elect a majority of each legislative house. Figures of this kind can be found in the National Municipal League's *Compendium,* as well as in the initial report on *Devaluation of the Urban and Suburban Vote* and in earlier research by Professor Manning Dauer of the University of Florida.[70] An inspection of these figures suggests an arithmetic truism that, even with all of the good will in the world, it is virtually impossible to construct a districting system in which 51 per cent of the voters will elect 51 per cent of the members of a legislative house. Some districts will always be under the average in terms of population, although they need not be far below. When the population in such districts is added, it becomes apparent that, even under an ideal districting scheme, the minimum percentage of the voters required to elect a majority in one house can rarely be as high as 47 or 48 per cent. But when the percentage slips below 45 per cent, it can be suspected that there is substantial room for improvement in achieving reasonable equality of representation in the districting plan.

A 45 per cent criterion would seemingly be practical, and would merit consideration as a rule of thumb when districting plans are under examination for the extent to which they achieve reasonable equality of representation. Such a rule could be especially useful in looking for cumulative deviations that are directed against one category of voters.

In using such a rule or any other rule, there is no reason why aspects of geography that work against groups of voters in one house must also be allowed to work against them in the other. Towns, counties, and cities that receive under-representation in one house should so far as possible be placed in districts where they will receive a like amount of over-representation in the other. One of the major advantages of bicameralism and of the different districting patterns for the two houses that result is the fact that it makes this kind of equalization possible.

The practice suggested has been illustrated in the experience of Virginia and other states and is one that was directed by provisions embodied long ago in the Constitution of Tennessee. The provisions, still legally valid, are to the effect that if a county has at least two-thirds of the ratio necessary for a seat in the lower house, it shall receive the seat; but the representation thereby taken away from the more populous counties shall be compensated for as nearly as practicable in apportioning seats in the state senate.[71]

An offset rule presents no special difficulties in application and is, in fact, a convenience in situations where population is intended as the standard for representation in both houses. It is often the only way by which voters in all parts of a state can be brought close to actual equality of representation in the state legislature as a whole.

Single- v. Multi-Member Districts

A third major issue is that of single-member versus multi-member districts. This issue has not been prominent in the recent proceedings in the courts, so far as can be learned from the available opinions, but it is inherent in all the situations where urban counties are being accorded large increases in representation. Historically, the issue has been acutely controversial in legislatures in this country and elsewhere since the middle of the nineteenth century, when theories favoring the use of single-member districts began to be widely held. The issue is also one much discussed by political scientists, although the existing state of knowledge in regard to relevant factors leaves much to be desired.[72]

Political scientists generally have been under the impression that the use of multi-member districts has not been common in electing state legislatures. In 1955, Professor Maurice Klain listed 17 contemporary textbooks in one footnote, and more in another, that asserted or implied the infrequency of the multi-member district. He found no outstanding authority who took a contrary position. Yet, he discovered, only 9 states chose all of their state legislators in single-member elections, and 45 per cent of all lower house members were being chosen in 1954 from multi-member districts. Klain reviewed the arguments on the merits of the two kinds of districts that had accumulated in more than a century of discussion, and found no strong weight of the evidence on either side.[73]

Most political scientists nonetheless seem definitely to prefer a plan of single-member districts to any use of multi-member districts. The National Municipal League is apparently about to recommend single-member districts only in its forthcoming revision of the Model State Constitution, presumably in deference to professional opinion.[74]

The number of state legislators elected in multi-member districts has increased in recent years. A tabulation as of March, 1962, appears in Table 2. It discloses 2,704 lower house members from multi-member districts against 2,499 from a similar tabulation for 1950, and 305 upper house members against 301 in 1950.[75]

The factors leading to the existing array of multi-member districts can readily be summarized. When a county grows to the point where it is entitled to 2 members rather than 1 in the lower house, it is less troublesome to elect the 2 members from the county at large than to divide the county into two districts. This remains true as the number continues to grow; however, the complications of long ballot choice become apparent in their turn as the number of members assigned a county exceeds 4, 5, or 6. The tendency then is to divide the county into districts, which in turn may be either single-member or multi-member. Table 2 shows a total of 3,976 members from counties electing 2 or more lower house representatives; 1,436 were from the undivided multi-member counties, averaging about 3 per county; 1,411 were from single-member districts smaller than a county; and 1,129 were from multi-member districts smaller than a county and averaging between 2 and 3 members per district.

What may be a surprising aspect of the table is the number of multi-member districts that are also multi-county districts. The answer can be found in the facts of geography combined with the reluctance to cross county lines in forming districts. For example, 3 adjacent counties may have almost exactly the right population collectively as a 2-member district even though 1 county is too big and the others are too small to justify a single member for each. Anyone who has struggled to compose districts in a state of mixed terrain and varying population distribution can testify that it is far easier to adjust representation to population in the rural areas while following county lines if an occasional 2- or 3-member district can be provided than if single-member districts only are required.

The present trend of the judicial decisions is to increase the number of representatives assigned to the large urban counties and to reduce the number of rural counties that are allowed to retain a single representa-

TABLE 2

State Legislative Districts by Number of Single- and Multi-Member Districts and Number of Representatives from Each Category, All Fifty States, March, 1962[a]

Size of District in Relation to Size of County	Numbers of Districts		Numbers of Representatives		Total Numbers of	
	Single-Member	Multi-Member	Single-Member	Multi-Member	Districts	Representatives
Lower Houses in 49 States						
Smaller than county	1,411	451	1,411	1,129	1,862	2,540
Identical	1,480	468	1,480	1,436	1,948	2,916
Multi-county	288	53	288	139	341	427
Totals	3,179	972	3,179	2,704	4,151	5,883
Upper Houses in 50 States, Including Nebraska Unicameral						
Smaller than county	365	0	365	0	365	365
Identical	578	65	578	180	643	758
Multi-county	655	62	655	125	717	780
Totals	1,598	127	1,598	305	1,725	1,903

[a]Compiled from state documentary materials by the Bureau of Public Administration, University of Virginia.

tive. Both aspects of the trend will probably lead to an increasing use of multi-member districts, although the more important aspect of the situation is undoubtedly found in the large urban counties. The question is whether this tendency should be resisted through a stronger effort to secure single-member districting.

It seems clear that situations like that of Cuyahoga County, Ohio (Cleveland), which elects at large an 18-member delegation to the Ohio lower house, are not especially desirable. Aside from questions of one-party dominance and possible machine control, no voter is likely to be able to vote a ballot for 18 seats with any degree of discrimination in the general election, and still less so in a party primary.[76] On the other hand, the single-member constituencies into which all of New York City is divided are not very inspiring. One can wonder how many voters in New York City know what assembly district they live in, or who their representative is, or how he votes; there is almost no medium of communication other than the direct canvassing of the voters that is geared to a nondescript area as small as a New York City assembly district. In 1961, all 12 of the assembly members from the Bronx were Democrats, as were 21 of 22 from Kings, 14 of 16 from New York County, and 9 of 13 from Queens.[77] Some minority party representation was evidently provided, either because of or in spite of the gerrymandering that had gone into the districting pattern.

Multnomah County, Oregon (Portland), illustrates an intermediate course that may have special virtues under some circumstances. After the county had reached a level of 16 members in the Oregon lower house, it was divided into 5 districts, effective in the election of 1956, with 4 of the districts electing 3 members each and the remaining district electing 4 members.[78] In 1961, these districts were represented by 7 Republicans and 9 Democrats, although the 7 state senators elected at large from the same county to the Oregon upper house were all Democrats.[79]

The bits of experience just cited from three different metropolitan areas are intended to indicate possibilities rather than to suggest normal outcomes from the districting patterns illustrated. The fact is that the generalizations in existing publications in regard to what will happen under one districting plan rather than another, generalizations usually based on what is referred to as "common knowledge," are generalizations that do not rest at all on any adequately comprehensive review of recent state experience. A substantial research effort would be needed to achieve a well-founded assessment. Even then, there would be question about how much to rely on the experience of the past in the new situation brought on by *Baker* v. *Carr*, a situation which will contain safeguards not previously available.

So far as the present writers are concerned, the case for single-member districts seems weakest in the smaller metropolitan areas where counties of intermediate size will find themselves entitled to additional members of a legislative house but to not more than 4 or 5 in all. In such counties the advantages of political community and of ready lines of communication by local press and radio all seem to be on the side of the single-county multi-member district. The hazards of gerrymandering are avoided; and if the parties are sufficiently competitive, they can divide the delegation. On the other hand, when a county in the half-million or million population class is divided into 4 or 5 multi-member districts instead of 15 or 20 single-member districts, there will be opportunity for gerrymandering in either case, but the hazards to adequate representation would seem less when the districts are larger. The simpler districting pattern would be more open to public criticism, and would certainly be easier to review in court, if it becomes necessary to go to court.

This discussion can be summarized by saying that the case for a rigid insistence on single-member districting has not been proved. The authors believe that any district electing more than 4 or 5 members at large should normally be divided, but they see no harm in continuing indefinitely the policies of many states in which 2- and 3-member districts are widely used.

Some Final Comments on Amending State Constitutions

For the longer term, the decision in *Baker* v. *Carr* has opened a new hope of genuine state constitutional reform. After the first major effects of the decision have brought change in the composition of state legislative bodies, it will be much more possible than formerly to convene state constitutional conventions on a basis of fair representation—a basis that has not been available in most states since the end of the nineteenth century. It can also be assumed that the arrangements for electing delegates to state constitutional conventions will become directly subject to challenge under the doctrine of *Baker* v. *Carr*.[80]

Meanwhile, however, the problem of unrepresentative action to amend state constitutions has suddenly taken on new importance in the context of the present litigation. Defenders of the *status quo*, taken somewhat off balance in April and May, were rallying strongly in June, July, and August. In several instances their counterattack has taken the form of immediately preparing state constitutional amendments that would give ground somewhat from the former inequities, but would freeze a new formula into the state constitution by popular action in November, 1962. Obviously, the hope has been that if a new popular majority could be obtained for a compromise plan, it might stand up in court simply by virtue of the recency of popular majority action.

The Alabama case provided one of the earliest illustrations of the process. During an 18-day session in July, the legislature proposed amendments installing a federal plan under which each county would have received equal representation in the upper house, despite the variation in county population from 10,726 to 634,864. This provision was categorically rejected by the federal court on July 25 when it ruled that any such plan would be invalid under the Fourteenth Amendment and proceeded to install an alternative plan for the upper house.[81]

In Florida, the legislature's action on August 11 was in the form of a proposed constitutional amendment for action by the voters on November 6, under which, if approved, additional members would be elected in a special election before the convening of the legislature in 1963. Under the legislature's proposal, gross inequalities of representation would remain in both houses, although urban areas would receive more representation than at present. Unlike the action in Alabama, the federal court in Florida in a decision on September 5 has apparently permitted the amending scheme to go forward. Information is not yet available on whether the decision will be appealed.[82]

In Rhode Island, shortly after *Baker* v. *Carr*, the legislature before it adjourned on April 15, initiated a constitutional amendment increasing the size of the lower house. This amendment would have to be passed again by the legislature in 1963 before going to the voters; meanwhile, however, the state Supreme Court has ruled that it would be inadequate to meet the standard of the Fourteenth Amendment. The legislature was to come back into session on September 5 to consider the problem further.[83]

In Delaware, a three-judge federal court issued an opinion on July 26 in which it indicated its view that the provisions of the Delaware Constitution on representation are invalid, but delayed further action in order to permit the legislature to prepare revised amending proposals for submission to the voters. The court is said to have expressed a preference for an amendment that would clearly give the general assembly responsibility for redistricting while omitting any specific plan of representation from the amendment. The court indicated doubt whether a proposed federal plan amendment could prove compatible with the Fourteenth Amendment and implied its opposition to the submission of any plan to the voters by which representation in one house would be frozen.[84]

In Oregon, where the state Constitution can be amended by an initiative procedure, rural interests have initiated an amendment that would make the state senate *less* representative than it is now; this proposal will presumably be on the ballot in November unless some court enters an order to the contrary.[85]

In California, another initiative state, Supervisor Frank G. Bonelli of Los Angeles County has petitions on file in Sacramento by which a proposed amendment is intended to go on the ballot to increase the size of the California senate from 40 to 50 members.[86] This is an attempt to remedy an inequity by voter action, but there is obvious question whether Supervisor Bonelli may not be settling for too little in the light of the *Baker* v. *Carr* decision. In *Moss* v. *Burkhart*, the federal court said that ". . . the right asserted here cannot be made to depend upon the will of the majority."[87]

In Colorado, two different amending proposals are expected to be on the ballot in November as the result of initiative action; one proposal would provide for a federal plan, the other for a population standard in both houses. On August 10, a federal court reportedly delayed action until November 15 on suits seeking reapportionment of both houses.[88]

Prior to *Baker* v. *Carr*, the West Virginia legislature on February 8, 1962, approved a proposed amendment for the ballot next November, under which an existing constitutional provision for grouping low-population counties would be replaced by a minimum guarantee of 1 seat per county in the lower house. So far as is known, this proposal has not been attacked in court.[89]

In Nebraska, where the unicameral legislature has not reapportioned itself since it was first constituted in 1935, the legislature acted in 1961 to propose an amendment to the state Constitution to qualify the population standard by adding area factors. A pending action in federal court is seeking an injunction to prevent a vote on the proposed constitutional amendment, as well as a court order to force reapportionment on a population basis as the present Constitution requires. Hearings in court were scheduled for August 27.[90]

In Michigan, a state constitutional convention, almost unable to function on the issue of representation in the light of *Baker* v. *Carr* because of its own built-in unrepresentative character, completed its work on May 11. Apparently no effort was made to challenge the composition of the convention under *Baker* v. *Carr* while the convention was still sitting, and it remains to be seen whether the unrepresentative character of the convention will provide grounds in court for attacking the product that the convention proposes to have laid before the voters. The new Constitution would replace the 1952 provisions on upper house representation with an "area-population" plan giving more weight to urban interests, but still falling short of any standard of equal representation of population. Unless stopped by court order, the new Constitution will apparently go to the voters in April, 1963.[91]

These many attempts to amend state constitutions on a basis far short of full equality of representation give some indication of what might happen if the Supreme Court should come down on the side of Judge O. Bowie Duckett of the Circuit Court for Anne Arundel County, Maryland.[92] With any encouragement at all from the Supreme Court, there might be as many as 15 or 20 states in which further attempts would promptly be made to amend state constitutions on a basis highly adverse to urban interests. What the voters would do in such a situation would doubtless vary from state to state, but not impossible would be an ironical outcome in which *Baker* v. *Carr* might even increase the number of situations in which major inequities were frozen into state constitutions.[93]

Some of the pending cases may soon result in further rulings by the Supreme Court, in view of the questions that will need settlement before ballots can be printed for the elections of November, 1962. Whether or not such rulings are made, it seems likely that most of the major issues discussed here will reach resolution in one form or another before the summer of 1963. The results will be apparent in the nominations and elections of 1964, and in the state legislatures that convene in 1965.

NOTES

[1] 369 U. S. 186 (1962).

In one of the first law review articles coming after the decision, Professor Ruth C. Silva began by saying that *Baker* v. *Carr* is probably the most important decision of the United States Supreme Court since *Marbury* v. *Madison*, 1 Cranch 137 (1803). Those interested in the cases relevant to governmental regulation of the economic system might disagree, but Miss Silva may be right so far as the distribution of power within the governmental system is concerned. Ultimately, even the present decision may take its greatest importance from its long-range effects on legislative decisions affecting economic matters. Ruth C. Silva, "Apportionment in New York," 30 *Fordham Law Review* 581-650 (April, 1962).

For a law review article on the origins and implications of *Baker* v. *Carr*, written after the decision, see Robert G. Dixon, Jr., "Legislative Apportionment and the Federal Constitution," 27 *Law and Contemporary Problems* _____. (Part II of Symposium on Electoral Process forthcoming.)

Mr. Charles S. Rhyne, former president of the American Bar Association and counsel for the plaintiffs in *Baker* v. *Carr*, in an address at the annual meeting of the American Municipal Association, August 27, 1962, as reported in the *New York Times*, August 28, 1962, said that in the period since the decision on March 26, 1962, the following had occurred:

Fifty-three law suits had been filed in 31 states.

There had been 41 opinions by the courts in addition to many more orders and interlocutory decrees.

Special sessions of the legislature had occurred in 8 states to adopt reapportionment laws: Alabama, Delaware, Florida, Georgia, Maryland, Tennessee, Vermont, and Wisconsin.

At a joint meeting of the American Political Science Association and the National Municipal League in Washington, D. C., September 8, 1962, Mr. Rhyne repeated this accounting in substance and also said that "courts have directly or by implication invalidated state law or constitutional apportionments of legislatures in whole or in part in 16 states. . . ." (Mimeographed text of statement, p. 4.) The 16 states he listed include the 14 listed in the present study at page 2; he also included Colorado and Delaware. The existing situation in those states appeared somewhat more ambiguous than that in the other 14, on the basis of the information available to the present writers, although they have no doubt that the previous apportionments will be changed.

[2] Justice Clark illustrated his conception of what could constitute a "rational policy" underlying a state system by citing the Georgia unit system, and said in a note, "Georgia based its election system on a consistent combination of political units and population, giving six units to the eight most populous counties, four unit votes to the 30 counties next in population, and two unit votes to each of the remaining counties." 369 U. S. 186, 253, n.4 (1962).

[3] *Sims* v. *Frink*, 205 F. Supp. 245 (1962). See also 30 *U. S. Law Week* 2512 (April 24, 1962) and 20 *Congressional Quarterly Weekly Report* (cited hereafter as

CQWR) 967 (June 8, 1962). The full text of the opinion of April 14, 1962, on hearing of application for interlocutory injunction in *Sims* v. *Frink* is available in photocopy of the signed typescript as filed with the clerk of court in National Municipal League, *Court Decisions on Legislative Apportionment* (New York: 1962) (hereafter cited as NML photocopy of opinions).

This collection of opinions was issued by the National Municipal League on July 31, 1962, and contains opinions handed down at various stages of the proceedings in some 13 cases involving 12 states, most of which opinions were not yet available in the regular reports as of July, 1962. In most instances the reproduction is from typescript. The collection lacks continuous pagination and therefore cannot readily be cited as a published volume of law reports; it preserves the original pagination of the opinions as photocopied in New York from what was in many cases a local photocopy of the original document. Some of the items include *graffiti* inscribed by Mr. Richard S. Childs before the decision was made to reproduce the collection. A second compilation of a similar character was issued at the beginning of September, 1962, and is hereafter cited as NML photocopy of opinions, Vol. II.

[4] *Toombs* v. *Fortson*, 205 F. Supp. 248 (1962); NML photocopy of opinion of May 25, 1962. See also 30 *U. S. Law Week* 2605 (June 12, 1962) and 20 *CQWR* 968 (June 8, 1962).

[5] *Baker* v. *Carr*,_____ F. Supp._____ (1962); NML photocopy of opinion of June 22, 1962. See also 31 *U. S. Law Week* 2003 (July 3, 1962) and 20 *CQWR* 1098 (June 29, 1962).

[6] *Sobel* v. *Adams*, 205 F. Supp., preliminary print no. 3, blue pages, p. 4; NML photocopy of opinions, Vol. II, for interlocutory judgment and opinion of July 23, 1962; 20 *CQWR* 1304, 1375 (August 3, 17, 1962).

[7] *Moss* v. *Burkhart*, _____ F. Supp. _____ (1962); see 181 A. 2d, preliminary print no. 5, blue pages, p. 1; NML photocopy of interlocutory decree and opinion of federal court, June 19, 1962, in which the case is evidently incorrectly identified as *Burkhart* v. *Rasberry*. Opinion of August 3, 1962, reported without identification of parties in 20 *CQWR* 1375 (August 17, 1962).

[8] *Mikell* v. *Rousseau*, NML photocopy of opinions, Vol. II. The decision of the Vermont Supreme Court, July 19, 1962, vacating a lower court decree of February 16, 1962, was reported in 20 *CQWR* 1305 (August 3, 1962). The Vermont Supreme Court is said to have ruled that the current apportionment of the state senate is unconstitutional and of no force and effect, but permitted time for action by the state legislature. On August 2 the state senate rejected a lower house bill apportioning the senate, but on August 9, by a vote of 15 to 13, the senate approved a senate reapportionment plan. The legislature then created a study commission of 3 senators and 3 house members to report in March, 1962, on the possibility of a revision of the state's apportionment. *Ibid.*, 1416 (August 24, 1962).

[9] The decision of the Rhode Island Supreme Court of July 24, 1962, ruling that the existing apportionment of the lower house was "invidiously discriminatory" and violated the Fourteenth Amendment was reported in 20 *CQWR* 1306 (August 3, 1962). The Rhode Island Supreme Court reportedly permitted further time for the state legislature to act and also noted probable rulings in a pending federal court

action; the state court also noted the probable invalidity under the Fourteenth Amendment of a pending amendment to the state Constitution. See also note 83 below. The NML photocopy of opinions, Vol. II, includes the opinion of July 24, 1962, noted above; the parties were *Sweeney* v. *Notte*.

10 *Maryland Committee for Fair Representation* v. *Tawes*, 180 A. 2d 656 (1962); NML photocopy of opinion of April 25, 1962, Maryland Court of Appeals; NML photocopies of opinions of May 24 and June 28, 1962, Circuit Court for Anne Arundel County. See also 30 *U. S. Law Week* 2522, 2587 (May 1 and June 5, 1962) and 31 *ibid.*, 2016 (July 10, 1962); 20 *CQWR* 969, 1150, 1304 (June 8, July 6, August 3, 1962).

11 *Scholle* v. *Hare*, 369 U. S. 429 (1962); NML photocopy of U. S. Supreme Court opinion of April 23, 1962; NML photocopies of decision and opinions of Michigan Supreme Court, July 18, 1962. See also the relatively full account of the hearing before Supreme Court Justice Potter Stewart when he granted the stay on July 27, 1962, as reported in 20 *CQWR* 1302-04 (August 3, 1962).

12 *Harris* v. *Shanahan*, NML photocopy of opinion of District Court of Shawnee County, Kansas, May 31, 1962. See also 20 *CQWR* 971 (June 8, 1962). A further decision by the District Court on July 26, 1962, and a stay entered by the Kansas Supreme Court on July 30, 1962, are reported in 20 *CQWR* 1306 (August 3, 1962).

13 *Lein* v. *Sathre*, 205 F. Supp. 536 (1962); NML photocopy of opinion of federal court, May 31, 1962. See also 20 *CQWR* 1071 (June 22, 1962).

14 *Fortner* v. *Barnett*, NML photocopy of opinion of Chancery Court of First Judicial District of Hinds County, Mississippi, undated, presumably decision of June 7, 1962, as reported in 20 *CQWR* 1071 (June 22, 1962). The opinion includes a complete plan of reapportionment that State Chancellor W. T. Horton said he would order if the legislature had not acted by November 24, 1962.

15 *Caesar* v. *Williams*, 371 P. 2d 241 (1962); NML photocopy of opinion of Idaho Supreme Court of April 3, 1962, as it appeared in 9 *Idaho Capital Report* 161; NML photocopy of opinion of Idaho Supreme Court in denial of rehearing, May 8, 1962, as it appeared in 9 *Idaho Capital Report* 201. See also 30 *U. S. Law Week* 2495 (April 17, 1962). The decision was on appeal from a lower state court decision in which it had been held that the 1951 and 1941 apportionment acts were unconstitutional and that the 1933 apportionment act should be brought back into effect. The Idaho Supreme Court reversed the lower court by a vote of 3 to 2, permitting time for the legislature to act. See also 20 *CQWR* 971 (June 8, 1962).

16 *Butcher* v. *Trimarchi*, NML photocopy of opinion, Court of Common Pleas of Dauphin County, Pennsylvania, June 13, 1962, in which the case is evidently incorrectly identified as *Start* v. *Lawrence*. The court declined to enter an immediate judgment that existing apportionment laws were invalid, but only on grounds that election procedures already in process for the present year should not be upset and that the legislature should have an opportunity to act in the light of *Baker* v. *Carr*. See also 20 *CQWR* 1071 (June 22, 1962).

17 The further decision of July 25, 1962 in *Sims* v. *Frink* was reported in 20 *CQWR* 1304 (August 3, 1962); on August 25, 1962, Supreme Court Justice Hugo L. Black refused to grant a stay in order to prevent special primary elections from

being held on August 28. *Washington Post*, August 26, 1962. The full text of the opinion of July 21 and decree of July 25, 1962, appear in NML photocopy of opinions, Vol. II.

[18] See note 5 above.

[19] See note 10 above.

[20] The quantitative measures of fairness referred to include especially the minimum percentage of the population of a state that can elect a majority of each house, but also include the average value of the vote in counties under 25,000 and between 25,000 and 100,000 population in contrast to the average value of the vote in counties of larger population categories. National Municipal League, *Compendium on Legislative Apportionment*, 2d ed. (New York: 1962); Paul T. David and Ralph Eisenberg, *Devaluation of the Urban and Suburban Vote* (Charlottesville: University of Virginia, Bureau of Public Administration, 1961), 3-10, 15, and state tables.

[21] See note 3 above.

[22] 20 *CQWR* 1304 (August 3, 1962).

[23] *Ibid.*; and see note 17 above.

[24] 203 F. Supp. 158 (1962). See also 20 *CQWR* 968 (June 8, 1962).

[25] 20 *CQWR* 1071 (June 22, 1962).

[26] Press comment in Georgia at the time was to the effect that if the district court decision stood, the kind of unit plan it would permit would not be worth the trouble even from the point of view of rural interests. Should the United States Supreme Court permit a more extreme form of unit plan than the lower court was prepared to countenance (which seems unlikely), some form of restoration might occur. But with the unit plan out of use for even a year, the political problem locally of securing any restoration before the next election year becomes more formidable, and especially if the legislature is being redistricted in the meantime—as also seems probable.

The appeal in *Sanders* v. *Gray* was filed before the United States Supreme Court had gone into recess for the summer of 1962. It may therefore be argued early in the October term and may be the first of the cases on appeal on which the Court provides a decision and an opinion on substantive issues.

[27] See note 4 above.

[28] 20 *CQWR* 1305 (August 3, 1962).

The information concerning the decision on September 6, 1962, was provided on September 8 by Mr. Charles S. Rhyne when he spoke at a joint meeting of the American Political Science Association and the National Municipal League.

An Associated Press dispatch, found later, indicates that the court reaffirmed its decision that at least one house must be redistricted before the meeting of the legislature in January, 1963. *Washington Post*, September 7, 1962.

[29] See note 5 above.

[30] See note 10 above.

[31] See note 11 above.

32 20 *CQWR* 1071, 1182, 1306, 1373 (June 22, July 13, August 3, 17, 1962). The names of the parties in this litigation were *State of Wisconsin* v. *Zimmerman*. The full text of the special master's report, in three parts dated July 25, July 31, and August 3, 1962, can be found in NML photocopy of opinions, Vol. II.

33 20 *CQWR* 1304 (August 3, 1962).

34 See note 6 above. Under the plan prepared by the legislature in August, which involves amending the state Constitution, the elections in November, 1962, would go forward as previously planned but if the voters approve enlarging the legislature to provide additional representation for urban areas, some 48 additional members would be selected at a special election to be held early in 1963. *Atlanta Journal and Constitution*, August 19, 1962.

The information concerning the decision of September 5 is from an Associated Press dispatch of that day from Miami, provided by the AP bureau in Washington, D. C. The court was quoted as saying, "If the constitutional amendment which the Florida legislature has submitted to the electors of the State for ratification or rejection . . . is ratified, the State will then have adopted a rational plan of reapportionment." Conversely, if the voters rejected the plan, then "further appropriate action can be taken by the Court, and jurisdiction will be retained for that purpose."

35 See note 7 above.

36 202 F. Supp. 741 (1962); NML photocopy of opinion of January 11, 1962; for the United States Supreme Court's opinion of June 11, 1962, see 370 U. S. 190 (1962); see also 30 *U. S. Law Week* 2361, 3383 (February 6 and June 12, 1962); *New York Times,* August 2, 18, 1962; 20 *CQWR* 1416 (August 24, 1962).

37 See note 11 above.

For pamphlets presenting contemporary discussions of the "federal" plan issue additional to that presented here, see Robert B. McKay, *Reapportionment and the Federal Analogy* (New York: National Municipal League, 1962) and Twentieth Century Fund, *One Man—One Vote* (New York: Twentieth Century Fund, 1962).

38 See note 11 above.

39 See note 11 above.

40 In his dissent in *Scholle* v. *Hare*, Supreme Court Justice John Marshall Harlan referred to the remand as "less than forthright," and as an "oblique invitation from this Court to hold that the Equal Protection Clause prohibits a State from constitutionally freezing the seats in its Senate, with the effect of maintaining numerical voting inequalities, even though that course reflects the expressed will of the people of the State," and concluded by saying, "I think dismissal is the right course." 369 U. S. 429, 434-35 (1962).

41 *Washington Post,* April 29, May 2, 1962.

42 See note 10 above.

43 20 *CQWR* 1304 (August 3, 1962), and other sources cited in note 10 above.

Mr. Royce Hanson of the Maryland Committee for Fair Representation reported at a meeting in Washington, D. C., September 8, 1962, that the plaintiffs were seeking a rehearing by the Maryland Supreme Court and in any event were being delayed in appealing to the United States Supreme Court because the Maryland Court had so far failed to issue an opinion supporting its decision of July 23, which was simply announced in court at the end of the day of argument.

On September 11, the Maryland Court refused a rehearing and promised an opinion within a week. *Washington Post*, September 12, 1962.

[44] See note 11 above.

[45] See particularly Gordon E. Baker, *Rural versus Urban Political Power* (New York: Random House, 1955), especially Chapter 2; Baker, *State Constitutions: Reapportionment* (New York: National Municipal League, 1960), especially pp. 3-5; James E. Larson, *Reapportionment and the Courts* (University: University of Alabama, Bureau of Public Administration, 1962), especially pp. 8-11.

[46] For a classification by Baker, based partly on one by Malcolm E. Jewell, see Baker, *State Constitutions: Reapportionment*, pp. 5-14. In an appendix of this publication, Baker also gives a concise statement of the provisions for each state as they existed in 1959. The authors have taken into account changes in some states since the Baker classification; in addition, their categories are somewhat different because of a desire to use categories more relevant to the issues in current litigation. Their information on state practice was further checked against the 1962 edition of the National Municipal League's *Compendium on Legislative Apportionment*, with which they are generally in agreement.

[47] These figures omit 5 states for which information is not available. They are based on the situation in 1962 prior to *Baker* v. *Carr* as reported by the National Municipal League in its revised *Compendium on Legislative Apportionment*, 1962. The criterion is the minimum percentage of the population that could elect a majority of each house; see also Paul T. David and Ralph Eisenberg, *op. cit.* in note 20, I, 4-7, and note 70 below.

[48] The Michigan story is amply reflected in the sources cited in note 11 above; see also Larson, *op. cit.* in note 45, pp. 70-75. On California, see Margaret Greenfield, Pamela Ford, and Donald R. Emery, *Legislative Reapportionment: California in National Perspective* (Berkeley: University of California, Bureau of Public Administration, 1959), especially pp. 37-42.

[49] See especially the opinions in the Georgia, Tennessee, and Alabama cases; but see also the views of the federal judges in Delaware, 20 *CQWR* 1305-06 (August 3, 1962), and Oklahoma, 20 *CQWR* 1375 (August 17, 1962).

[50] *Current Constitutional Issues*, Department of Justice mimeographed release of text of address prepared for delivery in Nashville, Tennessee, June 8, 1962, p. 3.

[51] The arithmetic value of each voter's vote for members of a state legislature can be computed as a percentage of what it would be if all voters had the same proportionate weight in the election of members of a state legislature. These values are available in the form of county averages for all states in the research studies by David and Eisenberg referred to elsewhere in this study. See note 20 above and p. 14.

[52] See note 45 above.

[53] Henry S. Commager, ed., *Documents of American History*, 3d ed. (New York: 1943), pp. 128-32 at 130. The Michigan plaintiffs in *Scholle* v. *Hare* cited the North-

west Ordinance and noted that Michigan Constitutions, beginning with the one of 1835, and continuing with those of 1850 and 1908, "wrote clearly the concept of representation based upon numbers. We insist this is a principle which is not subject to amendment." *Brief of Plaintiff, etc.*, by Theodore Sachs, undated, c. 1959 or 1960, mimeographed, at p. 28.

[54]William S. Carpenter, *Democracy and Representation* (Princeton, New Jersey: Princeton University Press, 1925), pp. 26-28, 31-33, 54-55.

[55]See note 7 above.

[56]New York state has a complex system of ratio rules in apportioning representation among the counties in both houses that has the effect of discriminating against the most populous counties and favoring those least populous. Ruth C. Silva, "Apportionment in the New York State Legislature," 55 *American Political Science Review* 870-81 (December, 1961), reproducing a document submitted by plaintiffs in the New York case of *WMCA* v. *Simon*, previously cited, note 36 above. Ratio rules are used in many states, especially in connection with minimums, less often as a part of a maximum rule or as a substitute for a maximum rule. Limits of space prevent any adequate discussion of the impact of ratio rules in the present study.

[57]See notes 24, 25, and 26 above.

[58]See notes 4 and 28 above.

[59]See note 6 above.

[60]See note 7 above.

[61]See note 10 above.

[62]See notes 3 and 17 above.

[63]20 *CQWR* 1375 (August 17, 1962).

[64]See note 12 above.

[65]Committee on Reapportionment of Congress, "The Reapportionment of Congress," 45 *American Political Science Review* 153-57 (March, 1951).

[66]The Celler bill was in the news in 1961 when Representative Celler said he would push the current version, H. R. 4068, because of the Republican gerrymandering of congressional districts in New York City. 19 *CQWR* 1869 (November 17, 1961). The present Congress was more preoccupied with the question of whether or not to increase the total number of seats in the House of Representatives, and seems not to have given serious consideration to districting standards. In 1959 hearings were held on the Celler bill, which was then 86th Cong., 1st sess., H. R. 73. See U. S. House of Representatives, Committee on the Judiciary, *Standards for Congressional Districts (Apportionment)*, Hearings . . . etc., June 24 and Aug. 19, 1959, Washington, D. C.: U. S. Government Printing Office, 1959.

[67]87th Cong., 1st sess., S. 2579.

[68]See *Sanders* v. *Gray*, 203 F. Supp. 158 (1962); 20 *CQWR* 968 (June 8, 1962). The electoral college analogy has been interpreted to the effect that in the electoral college on the basis of 1960 population data, New York has 85.5 per cent of the

representation it would be entitled to on a population basis; by analogy, it could be argued that no populous county should receive less than 85.5 per cent of the representation in a state legislative house to which it would be entitled on a population basis. *Cf.* A. B. Saye, "Court Assails Georgia County Unit Rule," 51 *National Civic Review* 317-18 (June, 1962).

[69] Silva, *op. cit.* in note 1, at p. 642.

[70] Manning J. Dauer and Robert G. Kelsay, "Unrepresentative States," 44 *National Municipal Review* 571-75, 587 (December, 1955), as corrected in Vol. 45, p. 198 (April, 1956).

[71] Tennessee Constitution, Art. II, sec. 6. See Legislative Drafting Research Fund of Columbia University, *Index Digest of State Constitutions*, 2d ed. (New York: Oceana Publications, 1959), p. 635.

[72] A brief but excellent discussion of the issue by Professor John H. Romani can be found in John P. Wheeler, ed., *Salient Issues of Constitutional Revision* (New York: National Municipal League, 1961), pp. 41-44.

[73] Maurice Klain, "A New Look at the Constituencies: The Need for a Recount and a Reappraisal," 49 *American Political Science Review* 1105-19 (December, 1955); footnotes referred to are note 4, p. 1106 and note 3, p. 1105.

[74] National Municipal League, *Compendium on Legislative Apportionment*, 2d ed. (New York: 1962); see blue sheet insertion in front matter.

[75] Figures relate to different years from those reported by Professor Klain, but are consistent for the lower house, where single-member elections are seldom held except in single-member districts. He found a considerably smaller number of "multi-election" state senators than the figures of the authors for state senators from multi-member districts.

[76] Professor John H. Romani comments as follows: "The author participated in four separate elections in that county (Cuyahoga) and, after each visit to the polling place, came away with a real sense of frustration. Although he knew many of the candidates through his work, he found it impossible to make intelligent choices in more than 50 per cent of the contests." In Wheeler, *op. cit.* in note 72, p. 42, n. 18. If a professional political scientist engaged full time in research on metropolitan area problems of the county in which he is living cannot keep track of the alternative candidates for 18 seats, it is indeed difficult to see how the average voter can do so.

[77] The breakdown of representation by counties was determined from the *New York Session Laws*, 1961. The source for party affiliation data was *Supplement I* of the 1960-61 edition of *The Book of the States* (Chicago: The Council of State Governments, 1961).

[78] Oregon *Laws*, 1955, c. 211, sec. 4.

[79] Oregon, *Journal of the Senate and House*, 1961.

[80] Mr. William J. D. Boyd of the National Municipal League, 47 East 68th Street, New York 21, N. Y., stated that he was unaware of any such action so far, in the course of a conversation by long distance telephone on August 27, 1962, during which he reviewed for the writers the status of amending proposals and pending litigation in most of the states discussed in this final section of the study.

34

In Tennessee, a suit is expected to be brought shortly, if it has not been already, to test the basis for representation in a state constitutional convention. The legislature made provision for such a convention at the same special session in 1962 in which it provided for reapportionment; representation in the convention would be on the basis that has prevailed hitherto in the Tennessee legislature. According to Mr. Charles S. Rhyne and Professor Robert J. Harris of Vanderbilt University, the mayor of Nashville has indicated that he will see to it that suit is brought to invalidate the proposed arrangements for electing delegates to the convention.

[81] 20 *CQWR* 1304-05 (August 3, 1962); see also notes 3 and 17 above.

[82] See notes 6 and 34 above.

[83] 51 *National Civic Review* 319-20 (June, 1962); 20 *CQWR* 1306 (August 3, 1962); see also notes 9 and 80 above.

[84] 20 *CQWR* 1305-06 (August 3, 1962).

[85] See note 80 above.

[86] 51 *National Civic Review* 375-76 (July, 1962).

[87] See note 7 above; the quotation is from p. 10 of NML photocopy of opinion of June 19, 1962.

[88] 51 *National Civic Review* 375 (July, 1962); 20 *CQWR* 1375 (August 17, 1962); see also note 80 above.

[89] 51 *National Civic Review* 211-12 (April, 1962); see also note 80 above.

[90] *New York Times*, August 26, 1962.

On September 12, 1962, the federal court refused to enjoin the vote on the proposed constitutional amendment and postponed action on redistricting. *New York Times*, September 13, 1962.

[91] 51 *National Civic Review* 373-75 (July, 1962), and prior reports on the Michigan convention; see also notes 11, 40, and 80 above.

[92] See note 10 above.

[93] The attention of the authors has been directed to this possibility most forcefully by their colleague who teaches constitutional law, Professor George W. Spicer of the University of Virginia.